MORE THAN A CONQUEROR

Message In A Moment
45-Day Devotional

CASONDRA BURKLEY

ISBN: 9781790359684

INTRODUCTION

This 45-day devotional is a collection of messages that I sensed God speaking to me in my own personal devotional time with him. I wrote these devotionals over a period of two years. I pray that each devotional will encourage you and challenge you to trust God, grow spiritually and learn tactics to shield yourself from the daily attacks of the devil.

The 15 extended devotionals are constructed from sermons that I have preached over the last 5 years.

I believe that as you read these daily devotionals you will be equipped to conquer the challenges of day to day life. I am prayerful that you will take time to meditate, pray and seek God's wisdom on how to apply each devotion to your life.

How to Approach This Devotional
M.A.P.

1. Meditate: Take a moment to read the scripture. Take a moment to read the full chapter of the bible the scripture is referenced from. Ask God how the particular scripture applies to you.
2. Apply: Read the devotion connected to the referenced scripture. Ask yourself what principles you can pull from the devotion to apply to your current situation or future situations.
3. Pray: Take a moment to journal your thoughts. After you have journaled, spend some time in prayer.

ABOUT THE AUTHOR

Casondra Burkley is a 40-year-old native of Houston, Texas. After graduating from James Madison High School, in 1997 she entered Baylor University, where she received her Bachelor of Arts Degree in Psychology and Speech Communications. It was during her sophomore year at Baylor that Casondra realized that God had a calling on her life. Casondra yielded to that call, and after graduation gave a year a half of her life to fulltime ministry with the Impact Movement, which is the sister organization to Campus Crusade for Christ. In 2006 she professed her call to preach the Word of God.

Casondra received her Master of Divinity at George W. Truett Seminary and a Master of Social Work at Baylor University, both in Waco, Texas in 2006. She has a plethora of experience in the field of social work, providing support, counseling, and guidance to children and adults in need. She has over 12 years of experience working as a licensed social worker. She currently works in the medical field of social work, helping children with special needs. She currently serves as the Co-Pastor of Fellowship of Faith Church, under the leadership of her husband Pastor David C. Burkley. They have one beautiful daughter.

Casondra loves writing plays, poetry, motivational speaking, and acting. She has acted in several plays and has graced the stage in numerous programs, banquets, conferences, and retreats. Casondra has offered workshops and seminars around the country. Casondra wrote and directed her first stage play "A Change is Gonna Come" in 2006, which resulted in her being honored by the Mayor of the City of Waco, with "Casondra Brown Day, May 6, 2006. Her love for the arts and speaking guided her in starting her own production company; Don't Wanna Miss Productions (DWMP). In 2016 she authored a book and released her second play, entitled Case Closed, based on her own true story of overcoming childhood poverty and a high school rape.

Birthed from her play and book is her latest development, Conquering the Obstacles of Painful Experiences (C.O.P.E. Inc.), a 501 (c) (3) organization which offers seminars, workshops, therapeutic and social services that assist individuals in taking what seemed to be a negative road block or obstacle in life and using it as a stepping stone to greatness.

Casondra's scripture to live by is Isaiah 6:8 "Also I heard the voice of the Lord. Saying whom shall I send, and whom will go for us? Then said I, Here I am; send me."

Visit her websites at:
www.morethancope.com
www.shipoffaith.com

To contact Casondra Burkley: send an email to
morethancope@yahoo.com

Please include your testimony or help received from this book when you write. Your prayer requests are welcome.

DAY 1

*10 The thief's purpose is to steal and kill and destroy.
My purpose is to give them a rich and satisfying life.
John 10:10 NLT*

Satan cannot create, he can only distort. He can only work within his limitations. He only goes after that which is good. If he is attacking you, there is something good within that area in which he is attacking that he desires to distort. Don't give in, don't give up. In the end, WE WIN!

JOURNAL

_____

_____

_____

_____

_____

_____

_____

_____

_____

_____

_____

_____

_____

_____

_____

_____

_____

_____

_____

_____

DAY 2

But Naaman became angry and stalked away. "I thought he would certainly come out to meet me!" he said. "I expected him to wave his hand over the leprosy and call on the name of the LORD his God and heal me! 2 Kings 5:11 NLT

So Naaman went down to the Jordan River and dipped himself seven times, as the man of God had instructed him. And his skin became as healthy as the skin of a young child, and he was healed! 2 Kings 5:14 NLT

How many of you are waiting on God to do something? When you look at the issues and His instructions, it doesn't make sense. For example when His instructions say stand still, but the issue says, make a move. God is sovereign. Even when His instructions don't line up with the issues, don't lose hope. Don't put God in the box of your logic. Just pray, listen, and be obedient. Your obedience is the bridge to your breakthrough.

JOURNAL

_____

_____

_____

_____

_____

_____

_____

_____

_____

_____

_____

_____

_____

_____

_____

_____

_____

_____

_____

_____

DAY 3

Wisdom shouts in the streets. She cries out in the public square. She calls to the crowds along the main street, to those gathered in front of the city gate: Proverbs 1:20-21 NLT

The woman named Folly is brash. She is ignorant and doesn't know it. She calls out to men going by who are minding their own business. Proverbs 9:13, 15 NLT

Many voices call out to us throughout the day, but it's up to us to choose which voice we will follow. Wisdom will call us to do things that are right; folly will call us to do things that are wrong. This battle is never-ending, but your choices will determine what path your life takes: emotionally, relationally, spiritually and physically.

JOURNAL

_____

_____

_____

_____

_____

_____

_____

_____

_____

_____

_____

_____

_____

_____

_____

_____

_____

_____

_____

_____

DAY 4

"When we were at Mount Sinai, the LORD our God said to us, 'You have stayed at this mountain long enough. Deuteronomy 1:6 NLT

What should have taken the Israelites 11 days, ended up taking them 40 years because of their wilderness mentality. Certain mentalities will keep you bound in the same situations, circumstances, and cycles until you allow God to transform your mind, these cycles will replay in your life like a broken record. From relationships to financial issues, change your perspective and watch your life change. Your mentality can be your dilemma, or it can be the bouncing board to your delivery. You have been at this mountain in life long enough; it's time to move.

JOURNAL

_____

_____

_____

_____

_____

_____

_____

_____

_____

_____

_____

_____

_____

_____

_____

_____

_____

_____

_____

_____

DAY 5

And we know that God causes everything to work together for the good of those who love God and are called according to His purpose for them. Romans 8:28 NLT

Troubled, frightened, discouraged, saddened, lonely, heartbroken, financially strapped, accused, mistreated, abandoned? Can you identify with any of these thoughts or feelings? We all face many emotional tests in our life, but tests are so much easier to take and pass when we've studied, and we know the answer; despite its level of difficulty. When you rely on the answers of life provided to us in the Bible, we can withstand and pass any test. The next time you take any of the tests above, remind yourself, God is working this for my good. We may not see it or even feel it, but it's working for our good.

JOURNAL

_____

_____

_____

_____

_____

_____

_____

_____

_____

_____

_____

_____

_____

_____

_____

_____

_____

_____

_____

DAY 6

Trust in the Lord with all your heart; do not depend on your own understanding.⁶ Seek his will in all you do, and he will show you which path to take.
Proverbs 3:5-6 NLT

When the children of Israel were headed to the promise land, God took them the long route. He knew if they faced certain obstacles they would go back to Egypt. God may be taking you the long route to ensure that you don't go backwards. God's instructions don't always make sense. But if you trust Him, He will lead you on a path to abundance.

JOURNAL

_____

_____

_____

_____

_____

_____

_____

_____

_____

_____

_____

_____

_____

_____

_____

_____

_____

_____

_____

_____

_____

_____

DAY 7

God is our refuge and strength, always ready to help in times of trouble. So we will not fear when earthquakes come and the mountains crumble into the sea. Let the oceans roar and foam. Let the mountains tremble as the waters surge! Psalms 46:1-3 NLT

Be still, and know that I am God! I will be honored by every nation. I will be honored throughout the world. Psalms 46:10 NLT

Going through storms in life is inevitable. We must remember storms do not last always. When you are in the midst of it, it seems like an eternity. In your storm, remind yourself not only will it soon cease, but most importantly, be still and know God is with you in the midst of it. Do not fear, God is in control.

JOURNAL

_____

_____

_____

_____

_____

_____

_____

_____

_____

_____

_____

_____

_____

_____

_____

_____

_____

_____

_____

_____

DAY 8

Though the Lord gave you adversity for food and suffering for drink, He will still be with you to teach you. You will see your teacher with your own eyes. Then the LORD will bless you with rain at planting time. There will be wonderful harvests and plenty of pastureland for your livestock. Isaiah 30:20, 23 NLT

Suffering and adversity are sometimes the result and consequence of our own decisions. However, even in the midst of this, God is still with us and waiting for us to get it right so that he can bring us into a place of peace and blessings. Unlike man, God's love for us is unwavering.

JOURNAL

_____

_____

_____

_____

_____

_____

_____

_____

_____

_____

_____

_____

_____

_____

_____

_____

_____

_____

_____

_____

DAY 9

Young people, it's wonderful to be young! Enjoy every minute of it. Do everything you want to do; take it all in. But remember that you must give an account to God for everything you do. Ecclesiastes 11:9 NLT

Every decision we make has consequences, whether good or bad. Don't let what you do today have a negative effect on what's in store for your tomorrow.

JOURNAL

_____

_____

_____

_____

_____

_____

_____

_____

_____

_____

_____

_____

_____

_____

_____

_____

_____

_____

DAY 10

Farmers who wait for perfect weather never plant. If they watch every cloud, they never harvest.
Ecclesiastes 11:4 NLT

What are you waiting on? If you are waiting for the circumstances to be perfect before you make a move in faith, you will be waiting forever. When God says move, take a step, stay, go, turn, yield, buy, sell, give, release, stop, that is not the time to weigh the options. Delayed obedience is disobedience and could cause you to miss your harvest. You say you are waiting on God for your harvest, and the reality is God may be waiting on you.

JOURNAL

_____

_____

_____

_____

_____

_____

_____

_____

_____

_____

_____

_____

_____

_____

_____

_____

_____

_____

_____

_____

DAY 11

*Even though the people were afraid of the local
residents, they rebuilt the altar at its old site. Then
they began to sacrifice burnt offerings on the altar to
the LORD each morning and evening.*
Ezra 3:3 NLT

Fear is a natural feeling that all people experience.
However, all people do not conquer their fear because
they allow it to immobilize their ability to make
decisions regarding finances, relationships, jobs and
more. Taking action is the only way to conquer fear!
What is it that you need to conquer today? Will you
join me as I take action?

JOURNAL

_____

_____

_____

_____

_____

_____

_____

_____

_____

_____

_____

_____

_____

_____

_____

_____

_____

_____

_____

DAY 12

Is your peace disturbed? If so, it is likely that you a Don't worry about anything; instead, pray about everything. Tell God what you need, and thank Him for all He has done. Then you will experience God's peace, which exceeds anything we can understand. His peace will guard your hearts and minds as you live in Christ Jesus. Philippians 4:6-7 NLT

Are you spending more time worrying than praying. The peace of God is a fortress to your heart and mind, which means they are protected. However, when you worry, your guard is down and you are in essence, carrying your problems instead of trusting God with them through prayer. Peace is priceless, don't become spiritually bankrupt by worrying.

JOURNAL

_____

_____

_____

_____

_____

_____

_____

_____

_____

_____

_____

_____

_____

_____

_____

_____

_____

_____

_____

_____

_____

DAY 13

*A prudent person foresees danger and takes
precautions. The simpleton goes blindly on and
suffers the consequences. Proverbs 22:3 NLT*

It is ok to say no and set boundaries for yourself. Do
not allow others to make you feel obligated to do
something in which you foresee any type of danger to
your emotional, physical, or spiritual wellbeing.

JOURNAL

_____

_____

_____

_____

_____

_____

_____

_____

_____

_____

_____

_____

_____

_____

_____

_____

_____

_____

_____

_____

_____

DAY 14

*"And now, dear brothers and sisters, one final thing.
Fix your thoughts on what is true, and honorable,
and right, and pure, and lovely, and admirable.
Think about things that are excellent and worthy of
praise." Philippians 4:8 NLT*

Painful memories of painful experiences often seem to rush in at inopportune times. It is imperative for all of us to practice thinking about what we think about. It is inevitable; if you think about negative things, you will have negative feelings. If you think about positive things, you will have positive feelings. Thinking about positive things will not make your problems disappear, but it sure makes it easier to cope with them.

Flashbacks from your past can do one of two things: immobilize you from fear or propel you forward to your purpose. The root of some flashbacks is the devil because he wants you to stay stuck in that painful place, whereas, other flashbacks remind you of just how great God is. Don't allow negative flashbacks of painful experiences to cause you to be stagnant! Push past the thoughts and focus on the positive.

JOURNAL

_____

_____

_____

_____

_____

_____

_____

_____

_____

_____

_____

_____

_____

_____

_____

_____

_____

_____

_____

_____

_____

DAY 15

17 When Pharaoh finally let the people go, God did not lead them along the main road that runs through Philistine territory, even though that was the shortest route to the Promised Land. God said, "If the people are faced with a battle, they might change their minds and return to Egypt."18 So God led them in a roundabout way through the wilderness toward the Red Sea. Thus the Israelites left Egypt like an army ready for battle. Exodus 13:17-18 NLT

God does not always take us the easy and short route. Sometimes, the route is long, hard, and filled with obstacles. But those obstacles prepare us for what lies ahead! Don't give up on God just because your route is tough, hang in there. When you are leaving a place of bondage and heading to a place of blessing, there are some things you have to go through to get you ready for it! Be encouraged!

JOURNAL

_____

_____

_____

_____

_____

_____

_____

_____

_____

_____

_____

_____

_____

_____

_____

_____

_____

_____

DAY 16

²⁸ Bless those who curse you. Pray for those who hurt you. Luke 6:28 NLT

The Bible tells us that we should pray for the people who have hurt or wronged us. I'm a witness that this can be one of the hardest prayers that you will ever pray, but it is also one of the most freedom and peace-giving prayers that you will pray. When we pray for the people that have hurt us, we are basically releasing our desire to get them back and trusting God to recompense. Is there someone you need to pray for? Don't wait, do it now.

JOURNAL

_____

_____

_____

_____

_____

_____

_____

_____

_____

_____

_____

_____

_____

_____

_____

_____

_____

_____

_____

_____

_____

_____

DAY 17

"The LORD had said to Abram, "Leave your native country, your relatives, and your father's family, and go to the land that I will show you. I will make you into a great nation. I will bless you and make you famous, and you will be a blessing to others." Genesis 12:1-2 NLT

Sometimes, you have to leave some things and some people behind in order to get to the blessings that lie ahead.

JOURNAL

_____

_____

_____

_____

_____

_____

_____

_____

_____

_____

_____

_____

_____

_____

_____

_____

_____

_____

_____

_____

DAY 18

But the LORD said to Samuel, "Don't judge by his appearance or height, for I have rejected him. The LORD doesn't see things the way you see them. People judge by outward appearance, but the LORD looks at the heart. 1 Samuel 16:7 NLT

Don't be dismayed by people who have overlooked you because of your outward appearance or because of something about you they didn't like. God chooses based on the heart. David was least likely to be chosen as king, but God saw in him what no one else could!

JOURNAL

_____

_____

_____

_____

_____

_____

_____

_____

_____

_____

_____

_____

_____

_____

_____

_____

_____

_____

_____

_____

_____

_____

DAY 19

Give your burdens to the LORD, and He will take care of you. He will not permit the godly to slip and fall. Psalms 55:22 NLT

Worried, concerned, anxious, weary, lacking peace? Could be because you are carrying your problems instead of giving them to God. He already has it worked out for you. He's just waiting for you to give it to him.

JOURNAL

_____

_____

_____

_____

_____

_____

_____

_____

_____

_____

_____

_____

_____

_____

_____

_____

_____

_____

_____

_____

_____

DAY 20

And I am certain that God, who began the good work within you, will continue His work until it is finally finished on the day when Christ Jesus returns.
Philippians 1:6 NLT

Others may leave things or situations undone, but God will finish what He started!

JOURNAL

_____

_____

_____

_____

_____

_____

_____

_____

_____

_____

_____

_____

_____

_____

_____

_____

_____

_____

_____

DAY 21

Around midnight Paul and Silas were praying and singing hymns to God, and the other prisoners were listening. Suddenly, there was a massive earthquake, and the prison was shaken to its foundations. All the doors immediately flew open, and the chains of every prisoner fell off! Acts of the Apostles 16:25-26 NLT

Have you ever been in a situation and you felt like you were in prison? I definitely have. Sometimes, it's tough to see past the present. But, I have learned that when you take your focus off your situation and shift it upward, something supernatural happens. We must learn to praise even when we are in prison type situations. We are not praising because we enjoy the pain, but we are praising because we know there is a promise. God will break the chains in your life and often, He will do it suddenly, but you must shift your focus! Praise in your prison.

JOURNAL

_____

_____

_____

_____

_____

_____

_____

_____

_____

_____

_____

_____

_____

_____

_____

_____

_____

_____

_____

DAY 22

When I heard this, I sat down and wept. In fact, for days I mourned, fasted, and prayed to the God of heaven. Nehemiah 1:4 NLT

O Lord, please hear my prayer! Listen to the prayers of those of us who delight in honoring you. Please grant me success today by making the king favorable to me. Put it into his heart to be kind to me." In those days I was the king's cup-bearer." Nehemiah 1:11 NLT

It's okay to cry about situations. Some situations are so devastating all you have is tears. Emotions are real and should be expressed, however, don't get so engulfed in your emotion that you forget that God can handle any and all situations. When you face difficult circumstances, don't just cry out to God in despair, cry out to Him and ask Him to use you as a part of the solution and the plan to resolve the matter.

JOURNAL

_____

_____

_____

_____

_____

_____

_____

_____

_____

_____

_____

_____

_____

_____

_____

_____

_____

_____

_____

_____

Day 23

But I say, love your enemies! Pray for those who persecute you! In that way, you will be acting as true children of your Father in heaven. For He gives His sunlight to both the evil and the good, and He sends rain on the just and the unjust alike. Matthew 5:44-45 NLT

Have you ever been upset when God blesses someone who hurt you? That could mean that you haven't forgiven them. Holding on to past hurts only hinders your progress! God blesses who He chooses. Instead of pouting about what is inevitable, pray about what's in your heart.

JOURNAL

_____

_____

_____

_____

_____

_____

_____

_____

_____

_____

_____

_____

_____

_____

_____

_____

_____

_____

_____

DAY 24

This is the day the LORD has made. We will rejoice and be glad in it. Psalms 118:24 NLT

There will always be something you can complain about. But there will always be something to praise about too! Your words have power, use them wisely!

JOURNAL

_____

_____

_____

_____

_____

_____

_____

_____

_____

_____

_____

_____

_____

_____

_____

_____

_____

_____

_____

_____

DAY 25

Why am I discouraged? Why is my heart so sad? I will put my hope in God! I will praise him again— my Savior and" Psalms 42:5 NLT

Emotions are natural and should be expressed. However, we must make sure that we don't live in our emotions. When we experience grief or sadness, we must acknowledge it, accept it, deal with it properly, and let it go. God never told us not to feel down; He told us to praise Him and be thankful in our tribulation. You may not feel like praising at this moment, but you will praise again.

JOURNAL

_____

_____

_____

_____

_____

_____

_____

_____

_____

_____

_____

_____

_____

_____

_____

_____

_____

_____

_____

_____

DAY 26

Then Jonah prayed to the LORD His God from inside the fish. He said, "I cried out to the LORD in my great trouble, and He answered me. I called to you from the land of the dead, and LORD, you heard me!
Jonah 2:1-2 NLT

Sometimes, we have to go through dark places in life in order for God to show us his power to deliver us. Our dark places are only opportunities for God to show His omnipotence, omniscience, and omnipresence.

JOURNAL

DAY 27

Moses and Aaron were among His priests; Samuel also called on His name. They cried to the LORD for help, and He answered them. Psalm 99:6 NLT

O LORD our God, you answered them. You were a forgiving God to them, but you punished them when they went wrong. Psalms 99:8 NLT

God hears our cries for help, and he answers them. However, don't think that because God answers prayers and blesses us that there won't be consequences for wrong actions.

JOURNAL

_____

_____

_____

_____

_____

_____

_____

_____

_____

_____

_____

_____

_____

_____

_____

_____

_____

_____

DAY 28

4 Love is patient and kind. Love is not jealous or boastful or proud 5 or rude. It does not demand its own way. It is not irritable, and it keeps no record of being wronged. I Corinthians 13:4-5 NLT

Don't be bound by the wrongs done to you. Keeping records of the hurts only keeps you bound to your past. If you are constantly repeating the wrongs done to you, you cannot move forward. It creates an unhealthy storage of emotions that will eventually begin to affect all areas of your life. Is there a wrong you need to let go off today?

JOURNAL

_____

_____

_____

_____

_____

_____

_____

_____

_____

_____

_____

_____

_____

_____

_____

_____

_____

_____

_____

_____

DAY 29

Father to the fatherless, defender of widows— this is God, whose dwelling is holy. God places the lonely in families; He sets the prisoners free and gives them joy. But He makes the rebellious live in a sun-scorched land. Psalms 68:5-6 NLT

Many of us either come from a dysfunctional family or have dysfunctions in our family. Some have even been abandoned or neglected by family. I'm so glad that God is a father to the fatherless and He sends people in our lives that become family through Christ. Don't fret about family members who have turned their back on you. Trust God and thank Him that He places the lonely in families!

JOURNAL

_____

_____

_____

_____

_____

_____

_____

_____

_____

_____

_____

_____

_____

_____

_____

_____

_____

_____

_____

_____

DAY 30

Create in me a clean heart, O God. Renew a loyal spirit within me. Psalms 51:10 NLT

Remember when you point your finger three are pointing back at you. Sometimes, we can get so focused on God fixing someone else that we forget about what God is trying to do in us! Today, take time to ask God what He wants to do in you.

JOURNAL

_____

_____

_____

_____

_____

_____

_____

_____

_____

_____

_____

_____

_____

_____

_____

_____

_____

_____

_____

_____

DAY 31

And I am convinced that nothing can ever separate us from God's love. Neither death nor life, neither angels nor demons, neither our fears for today nor our worries about tomorrow—not even the powers of hell can separate us from God's love. Romans 8:38 NLT

Too many of us know too well the pain of being abandoned, devalued by someone, or even abused mentally, physically, or emotionally. These things can leave damaging scars, but God will never turn His back on us. His love is inseparable. Don't fret about the scars of your past; they are simply reminders that you made it and it was only by the grace and love of God.

JOURNAL

_____

_____

_____

_____

_____

_____

_____

_____

_____

_____

_____

_____

_____

_____

_____

_____

_____

_____

_____

_____

DAY 32

So I concluded there is nothing better than to be
happy and enjoy ourselves as long as we can.
Ecclesiastes 3:12 NLT

I was once told, "you don't make me happy". It is not someone else's responsibility to make you happy. Happiness is a choice. Stop placing unrealistic expectations on others and get the root of your own unhappiness.

JOURNAL

_____

_____

_____

_____

_____

_____

_____

_____

_____

_____

_____

_____

_____

_____

_____

_____

_____

_____

_____

DAY 33

Cling to your faith in Christ, and keep your conscience clear. For some people have deliberately violated their consciences; as a result, their faith has been shipwrecked. 1 Timothy 1:19 NLT

Never fail to listen to the inner voice that is warning you about a person, a thing, or a particular activity. God speaks to us through our conscience, and when we don't listen, we experience grave consequences. Don't reject your conscience; there is a reason you have that feeling.

JOURNAL

_____

_____

_____

_____

_____

_____

_____

_____

_____

_____

_____

_____

_____

_____

_____

_____

_____

_____

_____

_____

DAY 34

Stay alert! Watch out for your great enemy, the devil.
He prowls around like a roaring lion, looking for
someone to devour. 1 Peter 5:8 NLT

Don't ever get too comfortable, just like God has a plan; Satan does too. Satan will try to do all he can to get you off the plan God has for you, and if you don't stay on guard, you will find yourself in a battle you are not prepared for.

JOURNAL

_____

_____

_____

_____

_____

_____

_____

_____

_____

_____

_____

_____

_____

_____

_____

_____

_____

_____

_____

_____

DAY 35

But the angel said, "Don't be afraid, Zechariah! God has heard your prayer. Your wife, Elizabeth, will give you a son, and you are to name him John. You will have great joy and gladness, and many will rejoice at his birth. Luke 1:13-14 NLT

But now, since you didn't believe what I said, you will be silent and unable to speak until the child is born. For my words will certainly be fulfilled at the proper time. Luke 1: 20 NLT

Don't be dismayed or discouraged by your circumstances — the things God has promised you will be fulfilled at the proper time. If it hasn't happened, it is not yet time.

JOURNAL

_____

_____

_____

_____

_____

_____

_____

_____

_____

_____

_____

_____

_____

_____

_____

_____

_____

_____

_____

DAY 36

It is God's will that your honorable lives should silence those ignorant people who make foolish accusations against you.1 Peter 2:15 NLT

It is unfair and does not feel good when someone attacks your character and their accusations are complete lies. I have learned over time that trying to defend yourself against an accuser is a waste of time especially if you know you are living a life of integrity. Don't worry about the false accusations that people make against you. Continue to live a life that's pleasing to God, and he will silence them.

JOURNAL

_____

_____

_____

_____

_____

_____

_____

_____

_____

_____

_____

_____

_____

_____

_____

_____

_____

_____

_____

DAY 37

So Joshua spared Rahab the prostitute and her
relatives who were with her in the house, because she
had hidden the spies Joshua sent to Jericho. And she
lives among the Israelites to this day.
Joshua 6:25 NLT

God can use any vessel that's willing. Rahab was a prostitute, but her willingness to help the people of God helped to spare her and her families lives. Rahab was an unlikely candidate because of her past, but God saw past that. Don't allow your past to prevent you from pursuing your present opportunities. Her past did not prevent her from being a part of the lineage of Jesus.

JOURNAL

_____

_____

_____

_____

_____

_____

_____

_____

_____

_____

_____

_____

_____

_____

_____

_____

_____

_____

_____

_____

_____

DAY 38

The LORD will guide you continually, giving you water when you are dry and restoring your strength. You will be like a well-watered garden, like an ever-flowing spring. Isaiah 58:11 NLT

When you don't know which way to turn or you find yourself in a place of weakness, lean on God to restore you. People may let you down, but the help of God is ever flowing.

JOURNAL

_____

_____

_____

_____

_____

_____

_____

_____

_____

_____

_____

_____

_____

_____

_____

_____

_____

_____

_____

_____

_____

DAY 39

Look after each other so that none of you fails to receive the grace of God. Watch out that no poisonous root of bitterness grows up to trouble you, corrupting many. Hebrews 12:15 NLT

If you've ever had a cut, puncture, incision or any type of open wound you know that there are several things you must do in order for that wound to heal. The first and most important thing you have to do is wash and disinfect the wound removing all dirt and debris. This is the same process we have to go through when we are wounded emotionally. In order to allow healing in and keep bitterness out, we must remove the dirt by not replaying negative experiences over and over, having the 'what if' syndrome, and holding on to things that God wants us to let go of. If you have open wounds, wash them and apply the pressure of the word, bandage them with prayer, and never pick at the scabs.

JOURNAL

_____

_____

_____

_____

_____

_____

_____

_____

_____

_____

_____

_____

_____

_____

_____

_____

_____

_____

_____

_____

_____

_____

Day 40

Don't call me Naomi," she responded. "Instead, call me Mara, for the Almighty has made life very bitter for me. Ruth 1:20 NLT

Tragic life situations that leave you with no answers can sometimes, cause you to see yourself opposite of how God sees you. Naomi's name meant my delight, but after losing her husband and children, she wanted to be called bitter. Later in the book of Ruth, we see that she truly is God's delight and her joy is restored. Don't allow temporary discomforts to lead you to make permanent determinations.

JOURNAL

_____

_____

_____

_____

_____

_____

_____

_____

_____

_____

_____

_____

_____

_____

_____

_____

_____

_____

_____

_____

_____

DAY 41

Turn away from evil and do good. Search for peace, and work to maintain it. Psalms 34:14 NLT

Many things and people will try to steal your peace. Sometimes, peace doesn't just find you; you have to go after it. When you find it, you must maintain it by getting rid of anyone or anything that threatens to take it away. Something as small as a flat tire can steal your peace if you let. IF you let. Don't let anything or anyone stand in the way of your peace.

JOURNAL

_____

_____

_____

_____

_____

_____

_____

_____

_____

_____

_____

_____

_____

_____

_____

_____

_____

_____

_____

_____

_____

_____

Day 42

*The LORD who rescued me from the claws of the lion
and the bear will rescue me from this Philistine!"
Saul finally consented. "All right, go ahead," he said.
"And may the LORD be with
you!" 1 Samuel 17:37 NLT*

God has never failed to come through on a promise. His power to deliver you from whatever you are going through is greater than your problem. His power raised Lazarus, and His power is the reason we celebrate a risen savior today. Rest, trust, believe, and hope in His power! If He delivered you before, He can do it again.

JOURNAL

_____

_____

_____

_____

_____

_____

_____

_____

_____

_____

_____

_____

_____

_____

_____

_____

_____

_____

_____

_____

_____

_____

DAY 43

And "don't sin by letting anger control you. Don't let the sun go down while you are still angry Ephesians 4:26 NLT

It's okay to get angry, but don't let your anger control you. Anger is a real and necessary emotion. But anger out of control can hurt, damage, and even sever relationships. Don't repress or ignore your anger. Acknowledge it, express it properly, set a boundary if necessary, release and let it go.

JOURNAL

_____

_____

_____

_____

_____

_____

_____

_____

_____

_____

_____

_____

_____

_____

_____

_____

_____

_____

_____

_____

DAY 44

*From a wise mind comes wise speech; the words of
the wise are persuasive. Kind words are like honey -
sweet to the soul and healthy for the body. Proverbs
16:23-24 NLT*

What's in your mind will eventually come out of your
mouth. Negative thoughts equal negative words.
Positive thoughts equal positive words. Change your
thought process, and your words will change. You will
be amazed at how much better you feel when you are
thinking and speaking positively about yourself, your
past, present, and future!

JOURNAL

_____

_____

_____

_____

_____

_____

_____

_____

_____

_____

_____

_____

_____

_____

_____

_____

_____

_____

_____

DAY 45

Write this letter to the angel of the church in Philadelphia. This is the message from the one who is holy and true, the one who has the key of David. What he opens, no one can close; and what he closes, no one can open. Revelation 3:7 NLT

Don't worry about the doors that other people close in your life. The doors that matter, they have no control over.

JOURNAL

_____

_____

_____

_____

_____

_____

_____

_____

_____

_____

_____

_____

_____

_____

_____

_____

_____

_____

_____

_____

DAY 1
MAYDAY, MAYDAY, MAYDAY

Lamentations 3:52-60

52 My enemies without cause
Hunted me down like a bird;
53 They have silenced⌐me in the pit
And have placed a stone on me.
54 Waters flowed over my head;
I said, "I am cut off!"
55 I called on Your name, O Lord,
Out of the lowest pit.
56 You have heard my voice,
"Do not hide Your ear from my prayer for relief,
From my cry for help."
57 You drew near when I called on You;
You said, "Do not fear!"
58 O Lord, You have pleaded my soul's cause;
You have redeemed my life.
59 O Lord, You have seen my oppression;
Judge my case.
60 You have seen all their vengeance,
All their schemes against me.

"Mayday is an emergency procedure word used internationally as a distress signal in voice procedure radio communications. It derives from the French *venez m'aider,* meaning, "come help me ("Mayday")."[1]

Have you ever found yourself in a situation in which you felt distressed? A situation in which it seems that there is no way out and all you can do is cry out, "God come and help me." If you refer back to Jeremiah Chapter 38, you will find that Jeremiah was thrown into a pit by his enemies. Jeremiah was not thrown in the pit because he had done something wrong, but he was thrown in the pit because of his obedience to the call of God. Lamentations 3:52-56 gives us a glimpse of Jeremiah's response when he found himself in a mayday situation. We can learn a lot from Jeremiah. His story lets us know that being a willing participant in the plans of God does not always feel pleasant and pleasing, but it will eventually lead to spiritual prophet.

When we find ourselves in a mayday situation, simply put, we must C.R.Y.

Cry Out to God-Jeremiah called out to the Lord from deep within the pit with pleading and weeping. It does not matter where you are; you can cry out to God.

Rely on His Response-Jeremiah trusted God's voice that told him not to fear. We must trust the Word of God, and apply it to all situations.

---

[1] "Mayday", *Wikapedia: The Free Encylopedia.* Wikapedia: The Free Encylopedia, 23 November   2018. Web. 29 July 2012, en.wikipedia.org/wiki/Mayday#cite_note-0

Yield to His Position and Vengeance-Jeremiah yielded to God as the authority in the situation, believing that God would be his advocate and acknowledging that God sees all things, and will vindicate him. We must know that God is in control and He will bring us justice when we have been wronged.

Life Application Questions

1. In what ways have you been depending on your own strength or ability to get you out of mayday type situations?
2. Is there a situation in your life in which you need to C.R.Y.? If so, write it down, take a moment to pray and ask God to give you the faith and courage to trust Him with the situation.
3. What can you do the next time you find yourself in a mayday situation?

_____

_____

_____

_____

_____

_____

_____

_____

_____

_____

_____

_____

_____

DAY 2
WHEN GOD REMEMBERS

Genesis 30:22-24
*22Then God remembered Rachel, and God gave heed
to her and opened her womb. 23So she conceived and
bore a son and said, "God has taken away my
reproach." 24She named him Joseph, saying, "May
the LORD give me another son.*

There are times in our lives we experience pain, struggles, and obstacles, and we sometimes think that God has forgotten about us. We think we've done something to anger Him, and He has turned His back on us, but this is simply not true. It is a tactic of the devil to tempt us to think that God does not love us because of something we've done or that God has forgotten about us because there is something or someone else more important. I have found in times that it seems as God has forgotten about me are often the times that God is doing the most work on my behalf.

There is a story of a man named Jim Marshall, who played for the Minnesota Vikings. In 1964, he picked up a fumbled ball and began running for the end zone. He could not remember which way his team goal line was, and unfortunately, he started running in the wrong direction. He ran 66 yards to the wrong end zone and scored a safety which is two points for the other team. I'm sure Jim's coach at the time wished he had remembered which direction to run the ball. Unlike Jim, God never forgets what direction victory is in, and He will lead us on the path of victory every day. (*Tomasson*)[2]

The phrase "God remembers" occurs 73 times in the Bible. Every time God remembers, it means God will act for someone according to his covenant promises. In Genesis 30, Rachel thought God had forgotten about her. She was barren, meaning she was unable to have children. In this day and time, women were looked down on if they were not able to have children. When Rachel cried out to God, He remembered her and opened her womb. Genesis 30:22 is the first time that it is recorded that Rachel cried out to God instead of looking to her husband or someone else to fix the problem. Rachel gives us great insight that we should always look to God first to fix what every situation we may be facing. What was impossible with man, now became possible with God, because He remembered her. Rachel bore a son, and God removed her shame. Although Rachel didn't realize it, there was a greater purpose at work. Her focus was having a son; however, God's focus was having a deliverer. Rachel waited over 7 years before

---

[2] Tomasson, Chris. "Vikings: 50 years later, Jim Marshall's wrong-way run remains an NFL classic". *Twin Cities,* Pioneer Press, 17 October 2014, www.twincities.com

she gave birth to her son Joseph. During our waiting periods, it's easy to fall into the pit of despair and envy, but when we trust God's timing and plan, we are able to remain steadfast until God moves on our behalf. The birth of Joseph was a part of God's perfect plan and perfect timing. In Genesis 37, Joseph later becomes the head of the land of Egypt during a time when there was a famine. God uses Joseph to rescue and deliver his family from this famine. Whatever you are facing, trust God's plan and purpose. Know that God will remember you and when he does, He will answer, act and accomplish his will.

Life Application Questions

1. Is there an area in your life in which you feel that God has forgotten about you? If so, take a moment to pray and ask God for peace in this area.
2. What did you learn about God's purpose and timing from the story of Rachel and Joseph?
3. How can you apply this lesson to your situation?

_____

_____

_____

_____

_____

_____

_____

_____

_____

_____

_____

_____

DAY 3
I WANT TO BE FREE

2 Corinthians 10:3-6

3 For though we walk in the flesh, we do not war according to the flesh, 4 for the weapons of our warfare are not of the flesh, but]divinely powerful for the destruction of fortresses. 5 We are destroying speculations and every lofty thing raised up against the knowledge of God, and we are taking every thought captive to the obedience of Christ, 6 and we are ready to punish all disobedience, whenever your obedience is complete.

Have you ever been to a circus and wondered how in the world they get a 13,000-pound elephant to follow instructions. Elephants that will perform in circuses are often selected at very young ages. In order to train them, they secure them to a pole with a chain. Inevitably, the elephant tries to get away, however, after many attempts, it finally yields to the idea that it can only go as far as the chain will allow. The elephant becomes so accustomed to having the chain around it necks, that eventually, even if not tied to anything, just having the chain around its neck alone will cause the elephant to stand still and in place. (What Baby Elephants Can to Us About Human Freedom)[3]

For many of us, we do not recognize that we are much like the elephant. Many philosophies, thought processes, mentalities, and behaviors we were raised in have been like chains around our necks. We have become so accustomed to them that we do not realize we are bound, and God wants us to be free. The reality is we are in a battle every day, and Satan, our enemy wants us to remain captive. I'm not sure what chain you may be dealing with, but I do know God wants you to be free.

To be free, we must first understand what a stronghold is. Stronghold has a threefold definition: 1) a point of operation from where Satan can keep the unbeliever captive or the believer incapacitated. In this context, incapacitated means unable to act, respond, or the like 2) a faulty thinking pattern based on lies and deception 3) anything the devil can use to keep us from faith and obedience.

Is there an area in your life in which you feel captive? Do you have a negative thinking pattern about certain people or situations that are based on lies? Is there an area in your life in which you are not operating in faith and obedience? If so, you may have

---

[3] Ruben, Steven Carr. "What Baby Elephants Can Teach Us About Human Freedom". *Huffington Post*, Oath Inc., 11 January 2013, www.huffingtonpost.com

a stronghold. In order to get rid of a stronghold, we must do three things.

One, we must get in the right fight. John McArthur says, "Believers are not instructed in the New Testament to assault demons, but to assault demons with truth"(MacArthur, p. 1643). [4] If what you believe does not line up with the Word of God, it is a lie. So, getting in the right fight simply means searching for the truth in God's word to apply to your situation. Two, we must use the spiritual weapons of fasting and prayer. Carnal weapons will not help us to win a spiritual battle. For example, you cannot use alcohol to soothe your stress or revenge to mend your broken heart. Thirdly, we must take every thought captive that exalts itself against the kingdom of God. I would like to challenge you to think about, what you're thinking about. Negative thoughts bring negative feelings and behaviors. Positive thoughts fuel positive feelings and positive behaviors.

---

[4] MacArthur, John. *The MacArthur Bible Commentary.* Nashville: Thomas Nelson, 2005.

Life Application Questions

1. What defeating thoughts commonly come to your mind? Find two scriptures that apply to these thoughts, memorize them and pray them every time these thoughts occur.

2. Is there an area in your life in which you feel captive? Based on today's lesson, what steps can you take to be free?

_____

_____

_____

_____

_____

_____

_____

_____

_____

_____

_____

_____

_____

DAY 4
I'VE BEEN HERE LONG ENOUGH

Deuteronomy 1:6-9
6 "The Lord our God spoke to us at Horeb, saying,
'You have stayed long enough at this
mountain. 7 Turn and set your journey, and go to the
hill country of the Amorites, and to all their
neighbors in the Arabah, in the hill country and in
the lowland and in the Negev and by the seacoast, the
land of the Canaanites, and Lebanon, as far as the
great river, the river Euphrates. 8 See, I have placed
the land before you; go in and possess the land which
the Lord swore to give to your fathers, to Abraham,
to Isaac, and to Jacob, to them and their descendants
after them. ' 9 "I spoke to you at that time, saying, 'I
am not able to bear the burden of you alone.'"

After attending my grandmother's funeral, I decided to keep one of the plants. Anyone who knows me, knows that I do not have a green thumb, but I was determined to keep and nurture this plant. After having the plant for some time, I noticed, although I was watering it and allowing it to get some sun, it began to die. After doing some research and talking to a few people, I learned that in order for some plants to grow properly, they must be re-potted in a new and larger pot. That was the case for this plant; it had to be moved to a new pot in order to grow. Much like this plant, we must sometimes, move from one place to another in order to grow properly.

The book of Deuteronomy is a book of sermons that Moses delivered to the people of Israel as they camped east of the Jordan river on the plains of Moab. God told them to leave the mountain, but they wandered for 40 years. They stayed in a place that was never meant for them to dwell in. Moses is basically saying throughout the book of Deuteronomy; you have been wandering for 40 years now; it's time to go into the Promised Land.

This text teaches us three things that keep us in places we were never meant to dwell; 1) being afraid to enter unfamiliar territory, 2) listening to the wrong people, 3) the condition of our heart.

In Deuteronomy 1:21, God told them to go occupy the land, but He also told them not to be afraid or discouraged. In verse 22, Moses sends out scouts to view the land. The scouting is referenced in Numbers 13. Caleb believed they could conquer the land, but the other men did not. They return with a negative report. Deuteronomy 1:25-27 addresses the rebellion the children of Israel demonstrated against God's commands which indicates the condition of their heart was not healthy. We see later in Deuteronomy that when the Israelites decided to be obedient to

God's command, they were able to move from the mountain and conquer the land.

Is God leading you to do something that seems uncomfortable? Are the people around you encouraging you or discouraging you? What condition is your heart in? It's time to move forward, are you ready to be obedient?

Life Application Questions

1. In what area is God saying that you have been in this situation long enough?
2. Are you willing to take the necessary steps to move away from this place?
3. What step will you take today?

_____

_____

_____

_____

_____

_____

_____

_____

_____

_____

_____

_____

DAY 5
WHY AM I IN THE MANGER?

Luke 2:4-7, 10-12, 20

4 Joseph also went up from Galilee, from the city of Nazareth, to Judea, to the city of David which is called Bethlehem, because he was of the house and family of David, 5 in order to register along with Mary, who was engaged to him, and was with child. 6 While they were there, the days were completed for her to give birth. 7 And she gave birth to her firstborn son; and she wrapped Him in cloths, and laid Him in a manger, because there was no room for them in the inn.10 But the angel said to them, "Do not be afraid; for behold, I bring you good news of great joy which will be for all the people; 11 for today in the city of David there has been born for you a Savior, who is Christ the Lord. 12 This will be a sign for you: you will find a baby wrapped in cloths and lying in a manger." 20 The shepherds went back, glorifying and praising God for all that they had heard and seen, just as had been told them.

The lotus flower is one of the most beautiful flowers you will ever lay eyes on. Its external beauty is not it's only significance. I particularly love this flower because it is one of few flowers that actually grows in muddy water. It literally rises from the mud. The deeper its root go in the mud, the more beautiful the lotus flower blooms. Often times, we find ourselves in muddy situations not realizing that God is doing a work and with His power, He will help us rise, overcome and bloom in those muddy situations.

In our text, Mary, Joseph, and Jesus find themselves in a muddy situation. Mary and Joseph had been on a journey for several days. The distance they were traveling was about 65 miles. Ladies, can you imagine being pregnant and walking 65 miles? Men, can you imagine your wife, mother or sister being pregnant and walking 65 miles? At some point after arriving at their destination, Mary gave birth to Jesus. She wrapped him in cloths and placed him in a manger, because there was no room at the Inn.

Mary's situation helps us to see that even when we are following God and are in alignment with His plans for our lives, we are not exempted from uncomfortable circumstances. Here, we have Mary who has given birth to the savior of the world, and there is no room for them at the Inn. The savior of the world is now placed in a manger. The manger was a place where the animals of travelers were placed. Many of us would agree, this is no place for the savior of the world. I believe it is significant to note Jesus was not born in the manger, but placed there. Our uncomfortable circumstances often have intentional significance. We must always remember that there is purpose in the circumstances God allows us to be placed in.

Jesus was placed in a manger in Bethlehem, which means house of bread. In other words, it's a place where people's needs are met. Jesus's placement in the manger was representative of his ability to relate to all people no matter how rich or how poor. Again, there was purpose in his placement. Where has God placed you recently? Does it seem like it's muddy or in a new age manger? Have you considered that maybe God has placed you there because He wants to show you His power and purpose, and use you as an example of blooming in muddy water?

Life Application Questions

1. What circumstance or situation have you found yourself in that you have complained about? In what way can you apply today's lesson?

2. Based on the response above, did you do something to end up in this situation or do you sense that God has placed you there purposefully?

3. In what way has God bloomed you in muddy water or in what way are you expecting God to bloom you in muddy water?

_____

_____

_____

_____

_____

_____

_____

_____

_____

_____

_____

_____

DAY 6
UNLIKELY CANDIDATE

1 Timothy 1:12-13
*¹² I thank Christ Jesus our Lord, who
has strengthened me, because He considered me
faithful, putting me into service, ¹³ even though I was
formerly a blasphemer and a persecutor and a
violent aggressor. Yet I was shown mercy because I
acted ignorantly in unbelief;*

Have you ever thought that you were not good enough or had an experience that you felt disqualified you from achieving a certain goal? A situation in which everyone around you may have considered you an unlikely candidate? Johnny Fulton was run over at the age of three. His hips were crushed, his ribs broken and his skull fractured, but he later ran a half-mile marathon in less than 2 minutes. Walt Davis was totally paralyzed by polio when he was nine years old, but later became the Olympic high jump champion. Lou Gehrig was a clumsy ball player and boys in his neighborhood would not let him play on their team, and he was later entered into the baseball hall of fame. Saul in the Bible who was later renamed Paul was a blasphemer and a persecutor of Christians, but he later wrote over half of the New Testament. All of these individuals like me and you at some point were unlikely candidates.

Despite what others may not see in you, God sees something in you. Paul was very thankful that God considered him trustworthy and appointed him to serve. Not only that, God filled him with faith and love, which was exactly what he needed in order to accomplish the assignments that lied ahead. If you have made mistakes or have dropped the ball, do not worry, God will have mercy on you, just as he did Paul. Know that God will strengthen you and equip you to do any work that He has called you to do. I once heard a pastor say, God doesn't call the qualified, he qualifies the called.

Say this with me, NO MORE EXCUSES! Despite your past, everything you need to succeed God has given it to you. Moses was a murderer; God gave him a rod, David was an adulterer, God gave a sling, Samson was lustful, God gave him the jawbone of a donkey. We are all unlikely candidates in one way, shape or form, but God will equip you and use your story for his glory.

Life Applications Questions

1. What difficulty or challenge have you faced in life that has caused you to doubt whether or not you can still achieve a certain goal?

2. What gift or skill do you need from God in order to accomplish your goal?

3. What is your role in accomplishing your goal? Have you done your part? If not, what step can you take today?

_____

_____

_____

_____

_____

_____

_____

_____

_____

_____

_____

_____

DAY 7
I'M GETTING IT ALL BACK!

Joel 2:23-27

23 So rejoice, O sons of Zion,
And be glad in the Lord your God;
For He has given you the early rain
for *your* vindication.
And He has poured down for you the rain,
The early and latter rain as before.
24 The threshing floors will be full of grain,
And the vats will overflow with the new wine and oil.
25 "Then I will make up to you for the years
That the swarming locust has eaten,
The creeping locust, the stripping locust and the
gnawing locust,
My great army which I sent among you.
26 "You will have plenty to eat and be satisfied
And praise the name of the Lord your God,
Who has dealt wondrously with you;
Then My people will never be put to shame.
27 "Thus you will know that I am in the midst of Israel,
And that I am the Lord your God,
And there is no other;
And My people will never be put to shame.

2014 was one of the toughest years of my adult life.
I went through a divorce from an emotionally abusive

relationship; I was terminated from my job as an Executive Pastor because I chose divorce over staying in an emotionally abusive situation. I went from making almost 6 figures and living in an almost 4000 square foot house, to living in the spare room of a friend and living on a credit card. Have you ever been in such a low place and you thought to yourself or even said out loud, I can't stand to lose anything else, but life doesn't relent, life continues to throw blow after blow?

Though this was a devasting time, I had to take some time to self-reflect, and one thing that stood out is my own choices led me to the situation I was in, but by studying the word of God, I was encouraged to know that God can restore everything that I have ever lost if it is in His will to do so.

The book of Joel opens with the explanation of destruction by locusts because of the people's sin and failure to follow the precepts of God. The locust plague represented devastation and judgment from God because of the people's disobedience. The four types of locusts symbolized a progression of God's judgment on the people of Israel. Each locusts attack represented the locusts destroying what was left from the locust that was there before until nothing was left and the people were left desolate. The story of the locusts reminds us that even in desolate places, God can turn your situation around. Where there is great destruction, God can bring great deliverance. Where there is great captivity, God can bring freedom. Where there is a great famine, God can bear great fruit. Where there is a great drought, God can bring abundant rain. We can get it all back. In order to get it all back, you must repent from your sins, remember God's promises and rely on his power.

Repent from Your Sin-In order to be in the right position to receive what God wants to restore to you; you must repent of your sins. Joel 2:12-13. In verse 13, tearing your heart means you become so grieved that you have dishonored God that you will do whatever necessary not to return to that sin again. God does not want rituals and religiosity; He wants relationship and righteousness.

Remember God's Promises-God promises rain and restoration. The former rain prepares the seed, and the latter rain causes the seed to swell. The former rain plants the seed of peace, the latter rain, He will give you peace that passes all understanding. The former rain plants the seed of a blessing, the latter rain says He will bless you exceedingly, abundantly, more than you can ask, think or imagine. The former rain plants the seed of healing, the latter rain gives beauty for ashes, joy for mourning, garment of praise for the spirit of heaviness.

Rely on God's Power-Joel 2: 26-27, Only God can take a barren land and make it fruitful. When you rely on God's power and not your own, you may face devastation, but you will not be destroyed. God has the power to turn your situation around.

Life Application Questions

1. Have you faced a devastating situation before? How did you respond?
2. Based on today's lesson, how will you respond in the future?

_____

_____

_____

_____

_____

_____

_____

_____

_____

_____

_____

_____

DAY 8
TURNING AROUND FOR ME

Mark 5:21-23 ²¹ When Jesus had crossed over again in the boat to the other side, a large crowd gathered around Him; and so He stayed by the seashore. ²² One of the synagogue officials named Jairus *came up, and on seeing Him, *fell at His feet ²³ and *implored Him earnestly, saying, "My little daughter is at the point of death; please come and lay Your hands on her, so that she will⌐get well and live." ⁴¹ Taking the child by the hand, He *said to her, "Talitha kum!" (which translated means, "Little girl, I say to you, get up!"). ⁴² Immediately the girl got up and began to walk, for she was twelve years old. And immediately they were completely astounded.

My family faced many challenges over the year. One challenge I recall very vividly is the time my mom, sister and I lived in a shelter. I was about 8 years old. I had an accident and ended up needing stitches on my finger. My mom hurried to get me to the hospital, but her car would not start. We ended up calling a cab, but when we returned from the hospital, my mom was told by the shelter director, if she can afford a cab she can afford to live on her own. We were kicked out of the shelter and found ourselves homeless. I can only imagine my Bible reading and praying. Mom cried out to God and asked him to turn the situation around for our family.

In Mark chapter 5, Jarius' daughter was very ill to the point of death. He went to Jesus begging Him to turn the situation around for his daughter; he wanted her to be healed. In this particular passage, Jesus does not respond to Jarius; He just goes with him. It is important for us to remember that in times of silence during crisis, it does not mean that God is not able or unwilling to intervene. Prior to going with Jarius, Jesus stops to address the woman with the issue of blood that was just healed by touch the hem of His garment. I can only imagine that Jarius may have been a bit anxious knowing that his daughter is at the point of death and Jesus stops on his way to his house. Not only did Jesus stop and attend to the woman with the issue of blood, but Jarius also received a message telling him not to bother Jesus anymore because his daughter was now dead. Jesus now responds to Jarius and says, do not be afraid only believe. Jesus arrives at the home, and the little girl is healed.

It is important for you to trust God in the midst of waiting periods. It is equally as important not to be discouraged when God does something for someone else, while you are waiting on him to do something for you. We must follow the instructions that Jesus gave Jarius, do not be afraid, only believe. Only believe was a command from Jesus, encouraging Jarius to have the same faith he had when he came to Jesus initially in desperation. When Jesus gave these instructions, Jarius situation had gone from bad to worse. Jesus eventually turned the situation around for Jarius and his wife, in His way and His timing. Can you trust Him to do the same for you?

Life Application Questions

1. Is there a situation or circumstance that you need God to turn around for you? Does it seem like you are in a waiting period? What can you do while you wait that shows that you trust God?

2. What will your situation look like when it has completed turning around? Take a moment to write a faith proclamation about your situation.

_____

_____

_____

_____

_____

_____

_____

_____

_____

_____

_____

_____

DAY 9
WHEN GOD GIVES NO REPLY

Matthew 15:22-28

²² And a Canaanite woman from that region came out and began to cry out, saying, "Have mercy on me, Lord, Son of David; my daughter is cruelly demon-possessed." ²³ But He did not answer her a word. And His disciples came and implored Him, saying, "Send her away, because she keeps shoutinʲat us." ²⁴ But He answered and said, "I was sent only to the lost sheep of the house of Israel." ²⁵ But she came and began to bow down before Him, saying, "Lord, help me!" ²⁶ And He answered and said, "It is not good to take the children's bread and throw it to the dogs." ²⁷ But she said, "Yes, Lord;ʲbut even the dogs feed on the crumbs which fall from their masters' table." ²⁸ Then Jesus said to her, "O woman, your faith is great; it shall be done for you as you wish." And her daughter was healed at once.

I read a story of an 8-year-old girl named Tess. She overheard her parents talking about her brother who was very ill. Her parents had to move out of their house because her parents could not afford the house bills and the medications. They were told the only thing that could save him was a very costly surgery that they could not afford. As her parents talked, she overheard her father say to her mother in a tearful voice, the only thing that can save him now is a miracle. Tess hurried to her room grabbed her piggy bank and counted the money she had. It added up to $1.11. She snuck out of the house down to the pharmacy. The pharmacist was talking. She tried to interrupt, but the pharmacist gave no reply. She couldn't take it anymore and slammed the money on the counter. The pharmacist very agitated at this point ask, how can I help you? My brother is really sick and has something growing in his head; my daddy said only a miracle could save him; I want to buy a miracle, how much does it cost? He told her we don't sell miracles here. His brother who he was talking to said: "Take me to where you live. I want to see your brother and meet your parents. Let's see if I have the kind of miracle you need." That well-dressed man was Dr. Carlton Armstrong, a surgeon, specializing in neurosurgery. The operation was completed without charge, and it wasn't long until Andrew was home again and doing well.

Like Tess, the Syrophoenician woman in Matthew 5, needed a miracle. When she asked Jesus to heal her daughter who was possessed by demons, He gives no reply. There are two reasons we sometimes get no reply to our prayers; God is testing our hearts, and God is testing our faith. Please know that every accepted prayer is not an immediately answered prayer. This woman teaches us that persistence is the pathway to problem-solving. If God has not answered your request and He has not given you a reply, remain faithful and persistent. The move of God in your life is connected to your faith. So, even when it seems like nothing is happening, know that God is working behind the scenes.

Life Application Questions

1. How is your faith being tested? In what ways have your actions shown that you trust God? In what ways have your actions shown that you do not trust God?

2. What recent prayers have you prayed in which God has given no reply? What can you do differently while you wait?

_____

_____

_____

_____

_____

_____

_____

_____

_____

_____

_____

_____

DAY 10
I JUST DON'T UNDERSTAND

Proverbs 3:5-6
5 Trust in the Lord with all your heart
And do not lean on your own understanding.
6 In all your ways acknowledge Him,
And He will make your paths straight.

Why? Why? Why? Why do some marriages end in divorce? Why do some children grow up in poverty, while others grow up in wealth? Why do some perfectly healthy people sometimes die at an early age? I could go on and on with questions that we often ask why about, but in most cases, we never get the answer. We are left scratching or shaking our heads saying, I just don't understand.

When we have trust for someone, we are basically saying that we feel safe and secure. We are proclaiming that we have confidence in them. Solomon tells us in Proverbs that we are to trust God with all our heart, which means we must find confidence in His power, comfort, and ability, even when we don't understand the situation.

The idea of leaning in this text means to rest your weight against something to give you support. If we rest in our own understanding, we will falter, because there are just some situations and circumstances in life we will never understand. When we find ourselves in situations we just don't understand, we should pray and seek God's guidance. It's important that we seek God's guidance in all areas. The moment we begin to pick and choose which areas we will allow God to direct our paths in, is the moment we start leaning unto our own understanding. We must trust that God will direct us and give us clear direction. Leaning to your own understanding and not allowing God to direct your path is like driving to a new destination without using the GPS or asking for directions, because the path that you started on has some familiar scenery as a previous destination you have been too.

No matter what decision you are making or what circumstance you may be experiencing, trust God to order your steps and lead you in the right direction. Trust him to comfort you in brokenness, heal you from trauma, deliver you from bondage, give you peace in the midst of turmoil. Even when you don't understand why, know that God is behind the scenes working things out for your good.

Life Application Questions

1. Is there a situation that you are facing or have faced and you are asking God why and you have not received a response?
2. How can you show God that you are trusting him and not leaning to your own understanding?

_____

_____

_____

_____

_____

_____

_____

_____

_____

_____

_____

DAY 11
IT'S TIME TO STRETCH

*2 Kings 5:1 **5** Now Naaman, captain of the army of the king of Aram, was a great man with his master, and highly respected, because by him the Lord had given victory to Aram. The man was also a valiant warrior, but he was a leper.*

10 Elisha sent a messenger to him, saying, "Go and wash in the Jordan seven times, and your flesh will be restored to you and you will be clean."

A blind girl was caught in a fire on the tenth floor. She made it to her window, but couldn't see anything. She could smell the smoke and feel the heat from the fire, but she couldn't see anything. She heard the fireman say, "Jump, Jump". I'm scared to jump; I can't see. The fireman said, if you don't jump you're going to die. I'm scared to jump; I can't see. Then she heard the voice of her daddy, say, jump sweetie, I've got you. When she heard his voice, she said ok, daddy, I'll jump. At this moment when she heard the voice of her father, she was willing to stretch her faith and jump, knowing that her father was going to catch her. (Evans, 97) 5

Many of us like this girl, have found ourselves now or at one time or another in which we are or were in situation, that if we did not make a move something would die. Maybe not a physical death, but maybe the death of a dream, the death of financial stability, the death of a relationship that's already on life support, the death of having peace. We've found ourselves at a place in which God was telling us to do something that didn't make sense, but the reality is, if you don't do it, you or it might die.

Naaman was a great man, BUT, he was a leper. He was the captain of his army, highly respected, and most importantly, the Lord used him in battle. He had position and power, but he had a problem. He had influence and impact, but he had an issue. He had dominance and drive, but he had a dilemma. He had courage and competence, but he had a complication. He had strength and superiority, but he had a situation. He had authority and ability, but he had an affliction. In other words, he was anointed and called by God, but he still had situations in life in which he had to use faith. Naaman was told to go and dip in the Jordan River to be healed. The Jordan river was muddy and grimy. Within his own reasoning, he questioned the instructions of the prophet. Naman

---

5 Evans, Tony. *Tony Evans' Book of Illustrations.* Chicago: Moody Publishers, 2009. Print

felt that dipping in the Abanah and Pharpar river would be better than the Jordan, because the water was much cleaner. The Jordan was like sewer water, and the others were like Ozarka spring water. When God gives us instructions to do things that may not make sense, we must make sure that we have rode ourselves of pride and our own reasonings. When Naaman was obedient and dipped in the Jordan River, he was cleansed. Naaman had to stretch his faith and believe that he would be healed, despite the uncommon path he was given to take.

When it seems that you are being led to do something that does not make sense, God may be trying to stretch your faith. Your faith is like a rubber band. When you stretch a rubber band, it expands, however when it retreats, it is able to stretch even further the next time you try to use it. Once you stretch your faith, you're able to trust even more the next time.

Life Application Questions

1. What are in your life if God is trying to stretch your faith? Has God given you instructions that do not make sense?
2. What step can you take today to show God that you trust His instructions and believe the outcome will be great?

_____

_____

_____

_____

_____

_____

_____

_____

_____

_____

_____

_____

DAY 12
AN ENCOUNTER WITH CHANGE

Genesis 32:24-30
24 Then Jacob was left alone, and a man wrestled with him until daybreak. 25 When he saw that he had not prevailed against him, he touched the socket of his thigh; so the socket of Jacob's thigh was dislocated while he wrestled with him. 26 Then he said, "Let me go, for the dawn is breaking." But he said, "I will not let you go unless you bless me." 27 So he said to him, "What is your name?" And he said, "Jacob." 28 He said, "Your name shall no longer be Jacob, butᴶIsrael; for you have striven with God and with men and have prevailed." 29 Then Jacob asked him and said, "Please tell me your name." But he said, "Why is it that you ask my name?" And he blessed him there. 30 So Jacob named the place Peniel, for he said, "I have seen God face to face, yet myᴶlife has been preserved."

There is a story of a man who was drowning. The man was panicking and fighting the water. The lifeguard jumped in the water, and although he had the power to save the man, he allowed the man to continue to fight the water until he lost all his energy. The lifeguard had to wait for the man to lose his energy so that he could be still enough to be saved. If the lifeguard had not done this, it was very likely that both men could have drowned. Sometimes, God has to allow us to struggle in our own strength and get weak so that He can save or change us. God changes your situation when you are at a place of surrender. (Evans, 126) [6]

Jacob wrestled with God all night long. At the end of this wrestling, God changed his name from Jacob to Isreal. His name went from meaning deceiver to fighter. Sometimes, we have to give up who we are in order to become who God wants us to be. Like the man drowning, we have to get to a place of weakness, so we are no longer depending on ourselves, but we are completely dependent on God. God wanted to change Jacob's character and it was through the struggle that this change occurred.

One thing I love about this particular story is the angel of God blessed Jacob right there where the struggle happened. Often times, when we face a struggle, we lose hope and sometimes, think that God is not able to fix or fill our needs or wants, but one encounter with change can bring blessings right in the placed that at one time seemed would never produce anything. No matter what struggle you may find yourself in today, trust and believe that right there in the midst of that struggle God can bless you there, but

---

[6] Evans, Tony. *Tony Evans' Book of Illustrations.* Chicago: Moody Publishers, 2009. Print

you must yield to God and not try to fight the battle on your own.

Life Application Questions

1. What is it that God is wrestling with you about?
2. What is God trying to change about your character?

_____

_____

_____

_____

_____

_____

_____

_____

_____

_____

_____

_____

DAY 13
BUT THIS TIME I WILL PRAISE

Genesis 29:35
35 And she conceived again and bore a son and said, "This time I will ᴶpraise the Lord." Therefore she named him Judah. Then she stopped bearing.

My husband and I often go out to eat on Sundays. For a while, going out to eat on Sundays became a staple in our schedules. While many people are planning out what they are going to wear to church the next day, we are normally trying to figure out what we are going to eat after church. On a typical Sunday morning, there's no time to eat a full breakfast, because we are so focused on ensuring that Sunday runs smoothly, so after church you can imagine, our stomachs are growling. As we arrive at the selected restaurant, we waste no time in ordering. If you were raised by mothers like ours, you were always taught to say grace. Depending on how hungry we were, would determine how long the grace would be. If we were really hungry, you might just hear, thank you, Jesus. If we were extremely hungry, we were praying before the food even arrived. It dawned on me one day that sometimes, we can get so focused on the "what" of our blessings that we forget about the "who" of our blessings. We get so focused on getting to the meal that we may not take the necessary time to truly thank the one who has allowed the meal to be possible. I wonder if like our food, when it comes to our lives, we are so focused on getting what we want, that we forget to take time to praise the ONE WHO blesses us in the first place. I wonder if we are spending too much time asking the questions like, God, what's taking you so long? God, how are you going to get this done in my time? God, when will my blessing get here? Why isn't my order JUST the way I ordered it? And not enough time praising God for what He is doing, has done, and will do.

Here is Genesis 29, Leah is having a similar challenge, while waiting for what she wanted, which was to be loved by her husband, she loses sight of praising God. God noticed that Leah was unloved and He opened her womb so that she could bear children. During each of these births, Leah was still consumed with wanting her husband to love her the way he loved her sister Rachel. Each time she bore another son, she named him to reflect her pain. (See Genesis 29:32-34). In verse 35, she bore a son again and named him Judah, which means praise. This time, Leah did not name her son to reflect her pain, she named her son to reflect her praise. This is an indication that there was a shift in Leah's perspective. There was a shift from the "what" to the "who". Although Leah did not receive the love she wanted from her husband, she was able to experience love and blessings from God.

We see later in the scripture that Jesus comes from the lineage of the tribe of Judah.

When we lose focus on the "who" of our blessings, we may potentially miss the miracle and blessing that God is trying to bestow upon us.

It is important that we always remember to focus on the "who" of our blessings and not the "what" of our blessings. Although Leah did not receive the love she wanted from her husband, she was able to experience love and blessings from God.

When you find yourself in tough situations, do not lose sight of the "who". Take time to praise God and believe that the "what" God has in store for you is so much greater than you could have ever imagined.

Life Application Questions

1. Is it difficult for you to focus on the "who" of your blessings versus the "what" of your blessings? Why or why not?
2. Is there a situation you are facing that you need to stop and thank God and shift your focus? If so, stop right now and take a moment to give God thanks.

_____

_____

_____

_____

_____

_____

_____

_____

_____

_____

_____

_____

DAY 14
I DON'T CARE WHAT IT LOOKS LIKE: I BELIEVE GOD!

Romans 4:18-24

18 In hope against hope he believed, so that he might become a father of many nations according to that which had been spoken, "So shall your [a]descendants be." 19 Without becoming weak in faith he contemplated his own body, now as good as dead since he was about a hundred years old, and the deadness of Sarah's womb; 20 yet, with respect to the promise of God, he did not waver in unbelief but grew strong in faith, giving glory to God,21 and being fully assured that what God had promised, He was able also to perform.22 Therefore it was also credited to him as righteousness. 23 Now not for his sake only was it written that it was credited to him, 24 but for our sake also, to whom it will be credited, as those who believe in Him who raised Jesus our Lord from the dead,

There was a drought that happened in a farming community many years ago. All the crops were dying, and the town was being affected. The ministers scheduled an hour of prayer and told everyone in the town to bring an object of faith with them. They met for the hour of prayer and directly at the end of the hour of prayer, it began to rain. The people began to get excited and raise up their various objects of faith; there was one object that stood out amongst the rest, a 9-year-old child brought an umbrella. This object was very significant because it represented the child's faith that it would rain, even though she did not see any clouds and there was no sign of rain. Like this little girl, we have to put our faith into action and believe. (Evans, 98) [7]

Paul uses the story of Abraham to answer three powerful questions about faith and believing for us; when should you believe, what should you believe and why you should believe.

When should we believe?

We should believe at all times, especially when the situation looks hopeless and dead. There was no reason for hope, but Abraham kept hoping. Abraham was expecting a positive outcome. In fact, the longer Abraham waited for the promises of God, the stronger his faith became.

What should we believe?

We should believe God's promises. Abraham had perfect certainty that God would fulfill every promise

---

[7] Evans, Tony. *Tony Evans' Book of Illustrations.* Chicago: Moody Publishers, 2009. Print

made to him. If you do not know God's promises, here are a few for your tool belt:

- For the weak: "He gives strength to the weary and increases the power of the weak " Isaiah 40:29
- For the lost: "I will instruct you and teach you in the way you should go; I will counsel you and watch over you." Psalm 32:8
- For the troubled and fearful: " Peace I leave with you, my peace I give you. I do not give as the world gives. Do not let your hearts be troubled and do not be afraid." John 14:27
- For those in need: "But my God shall supply all your need according to His riches in glory by Christ Jesus". Philippians 4:19
- For those who don't know there purpose: being confident of this, that He who began a good work in you will carry it on to completion until the day of Christ Jesus Phil 1:6

Life Application Questions

1. Are you experiencing a drought in a particular area of your life? What faith object can you use to represent your expectation that God will respond in that area of your life?
2. Which promise listed above can you apply to the area in which your faith is being challenged?

_____

_____

_____

_____

_____

_____

_____

_____

_____

_____

_____

_____

DAY 15
HOPE FROM WHERE YOU ARE

Genesis 13:14-15
14 The Lord said to Abram, after Lot had separated from him, "Now lift up your eyes and look from the place where you are, northward and southward and eastward and westward; 15 for all the land which you see, I will give it to you and to your [a]descendants forever.

Have you ever found yourself in a situation that did not align with how you pictured it would turn out? When I went through my divorce at 36 years old, I never imagined I would be homeless, without a job and living on a credit card, especially not with three degrees, but there I was in a situation I never thought I would be in. Often times, in situations like this we tend to lose hope. Though it may sound cliché, I am a firm believer that if God brought you to it, he would bring you through it.

Here in Genesis Abraham has already heard the message from God telling him that he would become a great nation and that he would be blessed and his name would be made great, however, the current circumstances did not align with what God had promised. Abraham was challenged to hope from where he was, even though where he did not align with where God said he was going and what God said would manifest in his life.

It is imperative that when you find yourself in situations of this sort that you remind yourself that circumstances do not circumvent the "I Will's of God". The I Will's of God are his promises to us. God's I Will's are supported by His Omnipotence, God has unlimited power and is able to do anything. God's I Will's are also sealed with immutability, which means God does not change. God is changeless in his person, purpose, and character. He may use different methods, but his purpose and character always remain the same.

When you are hoping from where are, find confidence in the Bible of the manifestation of God's I Will's

- Genesis-I will bless you and make your name great
- Exodus-I will lead you to a land flowing with milk and honey
- Leviticus-I will give you peace in the land
- Numbers-I will come down and speak with you
- Joshua-I will be with you; I will not fail you
- Samuel-I will show you what to do
- Kings- "I have heard your prayer, I have seen your tears; behold, I will heal you.
- Chronicles-Solomon because you asked for wisdom I will give you riches and wealth

- Job-I will teach you wisdom
- Psalms-I will be with you in trouble
- Isaiah- I will strengthen you, surely I will help you, surely I will uphold you with My righteous right hand.'
- Jeremiah- For I will turn their mourning into joy and will comfort them and give them joy for their sorrow.

Life Application Questions

1. What do you do when you find yourself in situations that seem hopeless? Do your actions align with the belief that God will restore hope in the midst of hopelessness?

2. What can you do differently in situations that did not turn out the way you hoped? How can you apply God's I Will's to your current situation or to situations that may arise in the future?

_____

_____

_____

_____

_____

_____

_____

_____

_____

_____

_____

_____

WORKS CITED

Evans, Tony. *Tony Evans' Book of Illustrations.* Chicago: Moody Publishers, 2009. Print

MacArthur, John. *The MacArthur Bible Commentary.* Nashville: Thomas Nelson, 2005. Print

"Mayday", *Wikapedia: The Free Encylopedia.* Wikapedia: The Free Encylopedia, 23 November 2018. Web. 29 July 2012, en.wikipedia.org/wiki/Mayday#cite_note-0

Tomasson, Chris. "Vikings: 50 years later, Jim Marshall's wrong-way run remains an NFL classic". *Twin Cities,* Pioneer Press, 17 October 2014, www.twincities.com

Ruben, Steven Carr. "What Baby Elephants Can Teach Us About Human Freedom". *Huffington Post*, Oath Inc., 11 January 2013, www.huffingtonpost.com

Made in the USA
Columbia, SC
02 December 2022

72347328R00087